CONTENTS: STRAND 3

Whole Numbers: Multiplication

Whole Numbers: Multiplication

1.   9
    $\times$ 7

2. 233
    $\times$ 3

3. 117
    $\times$ 5

4. 39
    $\times$ 8

5. 3,756
    $\times$ 4

6. 2,763
    $\times$ 50

7. 2,937
    $\times$ 400

8. 57,291
    $\times$ 6,000

9.   76
    $\times$ 29

10. 2,925
    $\times$ 57

11. 7,638
    $\times$ 2,927

12. 9,101
    $\times$ 204

Whole Numbers: Multiplication

REMEMBER?

$$\begin{array}{r} 2 \\ \times\,3 \\ \hline \end{array} \;\boxed{\mathrm{II}}\; \begin{array}{r} 2 \\ 2 \\ +\,2 \\ \hline \end{array}$$

A

1.
$$\begin{array}{r} 2 \\ 2 \\ +\,2 \\ \hline \end{array}$$

2.
$$\begin{array}{r} 2 \\ \times\,3 \\ \hline \end{array}$$

3.
$$\begin{array}{r} 3 \\ +\,3 \\ \hline \end{array}$$

4.
$$\begin{array}{r} 3 \\ \times\,2 \\ \hline \end{array}$$

5.
$$\begin{array}{r} 1 \\ 1 \\ +\,1 \\ \hline \end{array}$$

6.
$$\begin{array}{r} 1 \\ \times\,3 \\ \hline \end{array}$$

7.
$$\begin{array}{r} 5 \\ +\,5 \\ \hline \end{array}$$

8.
$$\begin{array}{r} 5 \\ \times\,2 \\ \hline \end{array}$$

9.
$$\begin{array}{r} 6 \\ 6 \\ +\,6 \\ \hline \end{array}$$

10.
$$\begin{array}{r} 6 \\ \times\,3 \\ \hline \end{array}$$

11.
$$\begin{array}{r} 4 \\ 4 \\ +\,4 \\ \hline \end{array}$$

12.
$$\begin{array}{r} 4 \\ \times\,3 \\ \hline \end{array}$$

13.
$$\begin{array}{r} 2 \\ +\,2 \\ \hline \end{array}$$

14.
$$\begin{array}{r} 2 \\ \times\,2 \\ \hline \end{array}$$

15.
$$\begin{array}{r} 7 \\ 7 \\ +\,7 \\ \hline \end{array}$$

16.
$$\begin{array}{r} 7 \\ \times\,3 \\ \hline \end{array}$$

B

1.
$$\begin{array}{r} 9 \\ +\,9 \\ \hline \end{array}$$

2.
$$\begin{array}{r} 9 \\ \times\,2 \\ \hline \end{array}$$

3.
$$\begin{array}{r} 7 \\ +\,7 \\ \hline \end{array}$$

4.
$$\begin{array}{r} 7 \\ \times\,2 \\ \hline \end{array}$$

5.
$$\begin{array}{r} 3 \\ 3 \\ +\,3 \\ \hline \end{array}$$

6.
$$\begin{array}{r} 3 \\ \times\,3 \\ \hline \end{array}$$

7.
$$\begin{array}{r} 6 \\ +\,6 \\ \hline \end{array}$$

8.
$$\begin{array}{r} 6 \\ \times\,2 \\ \hline \end{array}$$

9.
$$\begin{array}{r} 4 \\ +\,4 \\ \hline \end{array}$$

10.
$$\begin{array}{r} 4 \\ \times\,2 \\ \hline \end{array}$$

11.
$$\begin{array}{r} 8 \\ 8 \\ +\,8 \\ \hline \end{array}$$

12.
$$\begin{array}{r} 8 \\ \times\,3 \\ \hline \end{array}$$

13.
$$\begin{array}{r} 9 \\ 9 \\ +\,9 \\ \hline \end{array}$$

14.
$$\begin{array}{r} 9 \\ \times\,3 \\ \hline \end{array}$$

15.
$$\begin{array}{r} 5 \\ 5 \\ +\,5 \\ \hline \end{array}$$

16.
$$\begin{array}{r} 5 \\ \times\,3 \\ \hline \end{array}$$

17.
$$\begin{array}{r} 8 \\ \times\,2 \\ \hline \end{array}$$

18.
$$\begin{array}{r} 8 \\ +\,8 \\ \hline \end{array}$$

Name _____   Date _____

Whole Numbers: Multiplication

REMEMBER?

5 |IIIII|
× 3 |IIIII|
|IIIII|

A

1. 2
× 2

2. 5
× 2

3. 7
× 2

4. 4
× 2

5. 3
× 2

6. 9
× 3

7. 3
× 3

8. 8
× 2

9. 6
× 3

10. 5
× 1

11. 7
× 3

12. 8
× 3

13. 4
× 3

14. 8
× 2

B

1. 5
× 3

2. 9
× 2

3. 0
× 3

4. 4
× 3

5. 6
× 2

6. 0
× 4

7. 3
× 8

8. 3
× 9

9. 2
× 7

10. 4
× 1

11. 2
× 4

12. 5
× 1

13. 2
× 5

14. 7
× 4

15. 8
× 4

Whole Numbers: Multiplication

REMEMBER?

$$4 \quad \boxed{||||}$$
$$\times\,3 \quad \boxed{||||}$$
$$\boxed{||||}$$

A

1. $\begin{array}{r} 5 \\ \times\,3 \\ \hline \end{array}$ **2.** $\begin{array}{r} 6 \\ \times\,4 \\ \hline \end{array}$ **3.** $\begin{array}{r} 2 \\ \times\,5 \\ \hline \end{array}$ **4.** $\begin{array}{r} 9 \\ \times\,4 \\ \hline \end{array}$

5. $\begin{array}{r} 8 \\ \times\,5 \\ \hline \end{array}$ **6.** $\begin{array}{r} 5 \\ \times\,4 \\ \hline \end{array}$ **7.** $\begin{array}{r} 5 \\ \times\,5 \\ \hline \end{array}$ **8.** $\begin{array}{r} 4 \\ \times\,3 \\ \hline \end{array}$ **9.** $\begin{array}{r} 6 \\ \times\,3 \\ \hline \end{array}$

10. $\begin{array}{r} 7 \\ \times\,4 \\ \hline \end{array}$ **11.** $\begin{array}{r} 8 \\ \times\,2 \\ \hline \end{array}$ **12.** $\begin{array}{r} 6 \\ \times\,5 \\ \hline \end{array}$ **13.** $\begin{array}{r} 7 \\ \times\,6 \\ \hline \end{array}$ **14.** $\begin{array}{r} 3 \\ \times\,7 \\ \hline \end{array}$

- -

B

1. $\begin{array}{r} 9 \\ \times\,5 \\ \hline \end{array}$ **2.** $\begin{array}{r} 2 \\ \times\,4 \\ \hline \end{array}$ **3.** $\begin{array}{r} 7 \\ \times\,4 \\ \hline \end{array}$ **4.** $\begin{array}{r} 4 \\ \times\,5 \\ \hline \end{array}$ **5.** $\begin{array}{r} 8 \\ \times\,4 \\ \hline \end{array}$

6. $\begin{array}{r} 3 \\ \times\,4 \\ \hline \end{array}$ **7.** $\begin{array}{r} 6 \\ \times\,2 \\ \hline \end{array}$ **8.** $\begin{array}{r} 4 \\ \times\,4 \\ \hline \end{array}$ **9.** $\begin{array}{r} 9 \\ \times\,3 \\ \hline \end{array}$ **10.** $\begin{array}{r} 7 \\ \times\,2 \\ \hline \end{array}$

11. $\begin{array}{r} 5 \\ \times\,5 \\ \hline \end{array}$ **12.** $\begin{array}{r} 5 \\ \times\,6 \\ \hline \end{array}$ **13.** $\begin{array}{r} 9 \\ \times\,7 \\ \hline \end{array}$ **14.** $\begin{array}{r} 8 \\ \times\,6 \\ \hline \end{array}$ **15.** $\begin{array}{r} 5 \\ \times\,7 \\ \hline \end{array}$

Name _____   Date _____

Whole Numbers: Multiplication

REMEMBER?
4
× 6
24

A

1. 8
  × 6

2. 5
  × 6

3. 2
  × 6

4. 0
  × 6

5. 5
  × 7

6. 8
  × 7

7. 2
  × 7

8. 0
  × 7

9. 9
  × 6

10. 7
  × 7

11. 9
  × 7

12. 3
  × 6

13. 6
  × 6

14. 6
  × 7

- -

B

1. 4
  × 7

2. 7
  × 6

3. 1
  × 6

4. 4
  × 6

5. 1
  × 7

6. 3
  × 7

7. 6
  × 6

8. 6
  × 7

9. 8
  × 6

10. 4
  × 7

11. 3
  × 6

12. 4
  × 6

13. 5
  × 4

14. 3
  × 8

15. 8
  × 8

Whole Numbers: Multiplication

A

1. $\begin{array}{r} 5 \\ \times\,8 \\ \hline \end{array}$	**2.** $\begin{array}{r} 6 \\ \times\,8 \\ \hline \end{array}$	**3.** $\begin{array}{r} 2 \\ \times\,8 \\ \hline \end{array}$	**4.** $\begin{array}{r} 0 \\ \times\,8 \\ \hline \end{array}$	**5.** $\begin{array}{r} 8 \\ \times\,8 \\ \hline \end{array}$
6. $\begin{array}{r} 9 \\ \times\,9 \\ \hline \end{array}$	**7.** $\begin{array}{r} 0 \\ \times\,9 \\ \hline \end{array}$	**8.** $\begin{array}{r} 2 \\ \times\,9 \\ \hline \end{array}$	**9.** $\begin{array}{r} 8 \\ \times\,9 \\ \hline \end{array}$	**10.** $\begin{array}{r} 5 \\ \times\,9 \\ \hline \end{array}$
11. $\begin{array}{r} 1 \\ \times\,8 \\ \hline \end{array}$	**12.** $\begin{array}{r} 9 \\ \times\,8 \\ \hline \end{array}$	**13.** $\begin{array}{r} 7 \\ \times\,9 \\ \hline \end{array}$	**14.** $\begin{array}{r} 3 \\ \times\,9 \\ \hline \end{array}$	**15.** $\begin{array}{r} 3 \\ \times\,8 \\ \hline \end{array}$

B

1. $\begin{array}{r} 9 \\ \times\,8 \\ \hline \end{array}$	**2.** $\begin{array}{r} 8 \\ \times\,8 \\ \hline \end{array}$	**3.** $\begin{array}{r} 0 \\ \times\,8 \\ \hline \end{array}$	**4.** $\begin{array}{r} 2 \\ \times\,8 \\ \hline \end{array}$	**5.** $\begin{array}{r} 4 \\ \times\,8 \\ \hline \end{array}$
6. $\begin{array}{r} 0 \\ \times\,9 \\ \hline \end{array}$	**7.** $\begin{array}{r} 2 \\ \times\,9 \\ \hline \end{array}$	**8.** $\begin{array}{r} 9 \\ \times\,9 \\ \hline \end{array}$	**9.** $\begin{array}{r} 6 \\ \times\,9 \\ \hline \end{array}$	**10.** $\begin{array}{r} 5 \\ \times\,9 \\ \hline \end{array}$
11. $\begin{array}{r} 8 \\ \times\,9 \\ \hline \end{array}$	**12.** $\begin{array}{r} 7 \\ \times\,9 \\ \hline \end{array}$	**13.** $\begin{array}{r} 7 \\ \times\,8 \\ \hline \end{array}$	**14.** $\begin{array}{r} 6 \\ \times\,8 \\ \hline \end{array}$	**15.** $\begin{array}{r} 1 \\ \times\,9 \\ \hline \end{array}$

Whole Numbers: Multiplication

1. $\begin{array}{r} 2 \\ \times 3 \\ \hline \end{array}$
2. $\begin{array}{r} 6 \\ \times 6 \\ \hline \end{array}$
3. $\begin{array}{r} 7 \\ \times 2 \\ \hline \end{array}$
4. $\begin{array}{r} 2 \\ \times 8 \\ \hline \end{array}$
5. $\begin{array}{r} 8 \\ \times 7 \\ \hline \end{array}$
6. $\begin{array}{r} 3 \\ \times 5 \\ \hline \end{array}$

7. $\begin{array}{r} 6 \\ \times 0 \\ \hline \end{array}$
8. $\begin{array}{r} 1 \\ \times 5 \\ \hline \end{array}$
9. $\begin{array}{r} 0 \\ \times 4 \\ \hline \end{array}$
10. $\begin{array}{r} 1 \\ \times 9 \\ \hline \end{array}$
11. $\begin{array}{r} 3 \\ \times 1 \\ \hline \end{array}$
12. $\begin{array}{r} 7 \\ \times 5 \\ \hline \end{array}$

13. $\begin{array}{r} 9 \\ \times 2 \\ \hline \end{array}$
14. $\begin{array}{r} 2 \\ \times 6 \\ \hline \end{array}$
15. $\begin{array}{r} 7 \\ \times 8 \\ \hline \end{array}$
16. $\begin{array}{r} 1 \\ \times 6 \\ \hline \end{array}$
17. $\begin{array}{r} 5 \\ \times 8 \\ \hline \end{array}$
18. $\begin{array}{r} 6 \\ \times 1 \\ \hline \end{array}$

19. $\begin{array}{r} 9 \\ \times 9 \\ \hline \end{array}$
20. $\begin{array}{r} 5 \\ \times 3 \\ \hline \end{array}$
21. $\begin{array}{r} 5 \\ \times 5 \\ \hline \end{array}$
22. $\begin{array}{r} 3 \\ \times 3 \\ \hline \end{array}$
23. $\begin{array}{r} 2 \\ \times 7 \\ \hline \end{array}$
24. $\begin{array}{r} 0 \\ \times 5 \\ \hline \end{array}$

25. $\begin{array}{r} 7 \\ \times 1 \\ \hline \end{array}$
26. $\begin{array}{r} 9 \\ \times 5 \\ \hline \end{array}$
27. $\begin{array}{r} 3 \\ \times 4 \\ \hline \end{array}$
28. $\begin{array}{r} 0 \\ \times 0 \\ \hline \end{array}$
29. $\begin{array}{r} 1 \\ \times 7 \\ \hline \end{array}$
30. $\begin{array}{r} 3 \\ \times 9 \\ \hline \end{array}$

31. $\begin{array}{r} 9 \\ \times 4 \\ \hline \end{array}$
32. $\begin{array}{r} 5 \\ \times 2 \\ \hline \end{array}$
33. $\begin{array}{r} 2 \\ \times 4 \\ \hline \end{array}$
34. $\begin{array}{r} 2 \\ \times 1 \\ \hline \end{array}$
35. $\begin{array}{r} 5 \\ \times 6 \\ \hline \end{array}$
36. $\begin{array}{r} 8 \\ \times 3 \\ \hline \end{array}$

37. $\begin{array}{r} 4 \\ \times 7 \\ \hline \end{array}$
38. $\begin{array}{r} 4 \\ \times 5 \\ \hline \end{array}$
39. $\begin{array}{r} 8 \\ \times 0 \\ \hline \end{array}$
40. $\begin{array}{r} 4 \\ \times 4 \\ \hline \end{array}$
41. $\begin{array}{r} 9 \\ \times 7 \\ \hline \end{array}$
42. $\begin{array}{r} 0 \\ \times 6 \\ \hline \end{array}$

43. $\begin{array}{r} 3 \\ \times 8 \\ \hline \end{array}$
44. $\begin{array}{r} 2 \\ \times 2 \\ \hline \end{array}$
45. $\begin{array}{r} 6 \\ \times 7 \\ \hline \end{array}$
46. $\begin{array}{r} 8 \\ \times 8 \\ \hline \end{array}$
47. $\begin{array}{r} 6 \\ \times 9 \\ \hline \end{array}$
48. $\begin{array}{r} 6 \\ \times 3 \\ \hline \end{array}$

Whole Numbers: Multiplication

1. 6
  × 5

2. 1
  × 3

3. 4
  × 8

4. 0
  × 1

5. 1
  × 8

6. 0
  × 8

7. 7
  × 7

8. 5
  × 4

9. 4
  × 3

10. 2
  × 9

11. 7
  × 4

12. 0
  × 3

13. 3
  × 6

14. 4
  × 9

15. 4
  × 0

16. 9
  × 6

17. 9
  × 3

18. 6
  × 4

19. 3
  × 2

20. 6
  × 8

21. 7
  × 0

22. 8
  × 1

23. 8
  × 6

24. 1
  × 4

25. 2
  × 5

26. 5
  × 1

27. 8
  × 5

28. 5
  × 7

29. 7
  × 9

30. 2
  × 0

31. 9
  × 8

32. 9
  × 0

33. 8
  × 2

34. 1
  × 1

35. 6
  × 2

36. 9
  × 1

37. 7
  × 3

38. 1
  × 0

39. 4
  × 2

40. 7
  × 6

41. 8
  × 4

42. 0
  × 2

43. 3
  × 7

44. 4
  × 6

45. 5
  × 9

46. 0
  × 7

47. 8
  × 4

48. 8
  × 9

Name _____ Date _____

Whole Numbers: Multiplication

REMEMBER?
31   31
$\times\,3$ $\times\,3$

A

1.	13 $\times\,3$	2.	12 $\times\,3$	3.	20 $\times\,4$	4.	32 $\times\,3$
5.	21 $\times\,3$	6.	44 $\times\,2$	7.	31 $\times\,3$	8.	33 $\times\,2$	9.	41 $\times\,2$
10.	10 $\times\,6$	11.	24 $\times\,2$	12.	23 $\times\,3$	13.	34 $\times\,2$	14.	40 $\times\,2$

- -

B

1.	42 $\times\,2$	2.	30 $\times\,3$	3.	22 $\times\,3$	4.	14 $\times\,2$	5.	21 $\times\,4$
6.	32 $\times\,2$	7.	11 $\times\,7$	8.	43 $\times\,2$	9.	31 $\times\,2$	10.	30 $\times\,3$
11.	20 $\times\,2$	12.	23 $\times\,2$	13.	30 $\times\,2$	14.	12 $\times\,4$	15.	22 $\times\,2$

Name _____   Date _____

Whole Numbers: Multiplication

**SKILL 2 • Practice
Page 2**

REMEMBER?
213   213   213
× 3   × 3   × 3

A

1. 210
    × 4

2. 211
    × 3

3. 121
    × 4

4. 232
    × 3

5. 124
    × 2

6. 424
    × 2

7. 411
    × 2

8. 132
    × 2

9. 122
    × 4

10. 203
    × 3

11. 121
    × 3

12. 101
    × 5

13. 243
    × 2

B

1. 432
    × 2

2. 302
    × 3

3. 123
    × 2

4. 132
    × 3

5. 150
    × 1

6. 220
    × 3

7. 233
    × 3

8. 122
    × 3

9. 444
    × 2

10. 210
    × 3

11. 134
    × 2

12. 140
    × 2

13. 130
    × 3

14. 232
    × 2

15. 402
    × 2

Whole Numbers: Multiplication • Skill 2

Copyright © Houghton Mifflin Company. All rights reserved.

Whole Numbers: Multiplication

REMEMBER?
213
× 3
?39

A

1. 130 ×2	**2.** 321 ×3	**3.** 411 ×2	**4.** 332 ×2
5. 333 ×3	**6.** 144 ×2	**7.** 222 ×3	**8.** 124 ×2	**9.** 230 ×3
10. 103 ×3	**11.** 123 ×3	**12.** 240 ×2	**13.** 213 ×2	**14.** 202 ×4

- -

B

1. 234 ×2	**2.** 120 ×2	**3.** 123 ×2	**4.** 121 ×4	**5.** 110 ×5
6. 423 ×1	**7.** 313 ×3	**8.** 121 ×3	**9.** 130 ×2	**10.** 333 ×2
11. 101 ×6	**12.** 212 ×3	**13.** 104 ×2	**14.** 213 ×3	**15.** 240 ×1

Name _____ Date _____

Whole Numbers: Multiplication

SKILL 3 • Practice
Page 1

REMEMBER?

$$\begin{array}{r} \overset{1}{3}\,8 \\ \times\,2 \\ \hline \end{array} \quad \begin{array}{r} \overset{1}{3}\,8 \\ \times\,2 \\ \hline \end{array}$$

A

1. $\begin{array}{r} 12 \\ \times\,6 \\ \hline \end{array}$
2. $\begin{array}{r} 15 \\ \times\,5 \\ \hline \end{array}$
3. $\begin{array}{r} 18 \\ \times\,3 \\ \hline \end{array}$
4. $\begin{array}{r} 15 \\ \times\,3 \\ \hline \end{array}$

5. $\begin{array}{r} 17 \\ \times\,4 \\ \hline \end{array}$
6. $\begin{array}{r} 19 \\ \times\,3 \\ \hline \end{array}$
7. $\begin{array}{r} 17 \\ \times\,5 \\ \hline \end{array}$
8. $\begin{array}{r} 15 \\ \times\,6 \\ \hline \end{array}$
9. $\begin{array}{r} 14 \\ \times\,6 \\ \hline \end{array}$

10. $\begin{array}{r} 18 \\ \times\,5 \\ \hline \end{array}$
11. $\begin{array}{r} 16 \\ \times\,6 \\ \hline \end{array}$
12. $\begin{array}{r} 19 \\ \times\,4 \\ \hline \end{array}$
13. $\begin{array}{r} 12 \\ \times\,8 \\ \hline \end{array}$
14. $\begin{array}{r} 13 \\ \times\,7 \\ \hline \end{array}$

B

1. $\begin{array}{r} 17 \\ \times\,3 \\ \hline \end{array}$
2. $\begin{array}{r} 18 \\ \times\,4 \\ \hline \end{array}$
3. $\begin{array}{r} 19 \\ \times\,2 \\ \hline \end{array}$
4. $\begin{array}{r} 16 \\ \times\,3 \\ \hline \end{array}$
5. $\begin{array}{r} 19 \\ \times\,5 \\ \hline \end{array}$

6. $\begin{array}{r} 16 \\ \times\,5 \\ \hline \end{array}$
7. $\begin{array}{r} 12 \\ \times\,5 \\ \hline \end{array}$
8. $\begin{array}{r} 13 \\ \times\,5 \\ \hline \end{array}$
9. $\begin{array}{r} 14 \\ \times\,3 \\ \hline \end{array}$
10. $\begin{array}{r} 15 \\ \times\,4 \\ \hline \end{array}$

11. $\begin{array}{r} 13 \\ \times\,6 \\ \hline \end{array}$
12. $\begin{array}{r} 14 \\ \times\,7 \\ \hline \end{array}$
13. $\begin{array}{r} 16 \\ \times\,4 \\ \hline \end{array}$
14. $\begin{array}{r} 17 \\ \times\,2 \\ \hline \end{array}$
15. $\begin{array}{r} 18 \\ \times\,2 \\ \hline \end{array}$

Whole Numbers: Multiplication • Skill 3

Whole Numbers: Multiplication

REMEMBER?
$\begin{array}{cc} 1 & 1 \\ 3\,7 & 3\,7 \\ \times 2 & \times 2 \end{array}$

A

1.	2.	3.	4.
$\begin{array}{r} 24 \\ \times 4 \\ \hline \end{array}$	$\begin{array}{r} 23 \\ \times 4 \\ \hline \end{array}$	$\begin{array}{r} 26 \\ \times 3 \\ \hline \end{array}$	$\begin{array}{r} 15 \\ \times 5 \\ \hline \end{array}$

5.	6.	7.	8.	9.
$\begin{array}{r} 48 \\ \times 2 \\ \hline \end{array}$	$\begin{array}{r} 28 \\ \times 2 \\ \hline \end{array}$	$\begin{array}{r} 36 \\ \times 2 \\ \hline \end{array}$	$\begin{array}{r} 45 \\ \times 2 \\ \hline \end{array}$	$\begin{array}{r} 26 \\ \times 2 \\ \hline \end{array}$

10.	11.	12.	13.	14.
$\begin{array}{r} 25 \\ \times 3 \\ \hline \end{array}$	$\begin{array}{r} 24 \\ \times 3 \\ \hline \end{array}$	$\begin{array}{r} 25 \\ \times 2 \\ \hline \end{array}$	$\begin{array}{r} 27 \\ \times 3 \\ \hline \end{array}$	$\begin{array}{r} 29 \\ \times 3 \\ \hline \end{array}$

B

1.	2.	3.	4.	5.
$\begin{array}{r} 28 \\ \times 2 \\ \hline \end{array}$	$\begin{array}{r} 29 \\ \times 3 \\ \hline \end{array}$	$\begin{array}{r} 35 \\ \times 2 \\ \hline \end{array}$	$\begin{array}{r} 38 \\ \times 2 \\ \hline \end{array}$	$\begin{array}{r} 39 \\ \times 2 \\ \hline \end{array}$

6.	7.	8.	9.	10.
$\begin{array}{r} 46 \\ \times 2 \\ \hline \end{array}$	$\begin{array}{r} 49 \\ \times 2 \\ \hline \end{array}$	$\begin{array}{r} 23 \\ \times 3 \\ \hline \end{array}$	$\begin{array}{r} 17 \\ \times 3 \\ \hline \end{array}$	$\begin{array}{r} 28 \\ \times 3 \\ \hline \end{array}$

11.	12.	13.	14.	15.
$\begin{array}{r} 18 \\ \times 4 \\ \hline \end{array}$	$\begin{array}{r} 47 \\ \times 2 \\ \hline \end{array}$	$\begin{array}{r} 19 \\ \times 4 \\ \hline \end{array}$	$\begin{array}{r} 23 \\ \times 4 \\ \hline \end{array}$	$\begin{array}{r} 16 \\ \times 5 \\ \hline \end{array}$

Name _____   Date _____

Whole Numbers: Multiplication

<table>
<tr><td colspan="2">

REMEMBER?

$\overset{3}{1\,1\,7}$	$\overset{3}{1\,1\,7}$	$\overset{3}{\mathbf{1}\,1\,7}$
$\times\ \mathbf{5}$	$\times\ \mathbf{5}$	$\times\ \mathbf{5}$

</td></tr>
</table>

A

1. 446
   $\times\ 2$

2. 218
   $\times\ 3$

3. 226
   $\times\ 3$

4. 217
   $\times\ 3$

5. 238
   $\times\ 2$

6. 225
   $\times\ 3$

7. 324
   $\times\ 3$

8. 115
   $\times\ 5$

9. 125
   $\times\ 3$

10. 216
    $\times\ 4$

11. 114
    $\times\ 5$

12. 126
    $\times\ 3$

13. 124
    $\times\ 3$

B

1. 225
   $\times\ 2$

2. 215
   $\times\ 4$

3. 116
   $\times\ 6$

4. 214
   $\times\ 3$

5. 123
   $\times\ 4$

6. 437
   $\times\ 2$

7. 217
   $\times\ 2$

8. 319
   $\times\ 2$

9. 325
   $\times\ 2$

10. 145
    $\times\ 2$

11. 215
    $\times\ 3$

12. 223
    $\times\ 4$

13. 138
    $\times\ 2$

14. 113
    $\times\ 7$

15. 118
    $\times\ 5$

Whole Numbers: Multiplication

REMEMBER?
$\begin{array}{r}4\\ 3\,7\\ \times\,7\\\hline\end{array}$ $\begin{array}{r}4\\ 3\,7\\ \times\,7\\\hline\end{array}$

A

1. $\begin{array}{r}32\\ \times\,7\\\hline\end{array}$ **2.** $\begin{array}{r}55\\ \times\,3\\\hline\end{array}$ **3.** $\begin{array}{r}46\\ \times\,3\\\hline\end{array}$ **4.** $\begin{array}{r}72\\ \times\,8\\\hline\end{array}$

5. $\begin{array}{r}97\\ \times\,5\\\hline\end{array}$ **6.** $\begin{array}{r}95\\ \times\,4\\\hline\end{array}$ **7.** $\begin{array}{r}57\\ \times\,3\\\hline\end{array}$ **8.** $\begin{array}{r}75\\ \times\,3\\\hline\end{array}$ **9.** $\begin{array}{r}89\\ \times\,2\\\hline\end{array}$

10. $\begin{array}{r}66\\ \times\,4\\\hline\end{array}$ **11.** $\begin{array}{r}38\\ \times\,4\\\hline\end{array}$ **12.** $\begin{array}{r}43\\ \times\,4\\\hline\end{array}$ **13.** $\begin{array}{r}67\\ \times\,7\\\hline\end{array}$ **14.** $\begin{array}{r}89\\ \times\,3\\\hline\end{array}$

B

1. $\begin{array}{r}69\\ \times\,9\\\hline\end{array}$ **2.** $\begin{array}{r}24\\ \times\,7\\\hline\end{array}$ **3.** $\begin{array}{r}86\\ \times\,8\\\hline\end{array}$ **4.** $\begin{array}{r}96\\ \times\,9\\\hline\end{array}$ **5.** $\begin{array}{r}77\\ \times\,4\\\hline\end{array}$

6. $\begin{array}{r}65\\ \times\,6\\\hline\end{array}$ **7.** $\begin{array}{r}89\\ \times\,3\\\hline\end{array}$ **8.** $\begin{array}{r}84\\ \times\,4\\\hline\end{array}$ **9.** $\begin{array}{r}79\\ \times\,2\\\hline\end{array}$ **10.** $\begin{array}{r}58\\ \times\,4\\\hline\end{array}$

11. $\begin{array}{r}32\\ \times\,9\\\hline\end{array}$ **12.** $\begin{array}{r}48\\ \times\,9\\\hline\end{array}$ **13.** $\begin{array}{r}56\\ \times\,8\\\hline\end{array}$ **14.** $\begin{array}{r}65\\ \times\,3\\\hline\end{array}$ **15.** $\begin{array}{r}97\\ \times\,3\\\hline\end{array}$

Whole Numbers: Multiplication

REMEMBER?

$$\begin{array}{cc} 2 & 2 \\ 2\,6 & 2\,6 \\ \times\,4 & \times\,4 \end{array}$$

A

1. $\begin{array}{r} 42 \\ \times\,8 \\ \hline \end{array}$ **2.** $\begin{array}{r} 65 \\ \times\,2 \\ \hline \end{array}$ **3.** $\begin{array}{r} 84 \\ \times\,8 \\ \hline \end{array}$ **4.** $\begin{array}{r} 67 \\ \times\,3 \\ \hline \end{array}$

5. $\begin{array}{r} 56 \\ \times\,4 \\ \hline \end{array}$ **6.** $\begin{array}{r} 96 \\ \times\,4 \\ \hline \end{array}$ **7.** $\begin{array}{r} 65 \\ \times\,6 \\ \hline \end{array}$ **8.** $\begin{array}{r} 73 \\ \times\,7 \\ \hline \end{array}$ **9.** $\begin{array}{r} 26 \\ \times\,8 \\ \hline \end{array}$

10. $\begin{array}{r} 92 \\ \times\,8 \\ \hline \end{array}$ **11.** $\begin{array}{r} 44 \\ \times\,6 \\ \hline \end{array}$ **12.** $\begin{array}{r} 37 \\ \times\,4 \\ \hline \end{array}$ **13.** $\begin{array}{r} 53 \\ \times\,5 \\ \hline \end{array}$ **14.** $\begin{array}{r} 82 \\ \times\,5 \\ \hline \end{array}$

B

1. $\begin{array}{r} 85 \\ \times\,3 \\ \hline \end{array}$ **2.** $\begin{array}{r} 39 \\ \times\,3 \\ \hline \end{array}$ **3.** $\begin{array}{r} 24 \\ \times\,8 \\ \hline \end{array}$ **4.** $\begin{array}{r} 55 \\ \times\,5 \\ \hline \end{array}$ **5.** $\begin{array}{r} 16 \\ \times\,9 \\ \hline \end{array}$

6. $\begin{array}{r} 33 \\ \times\,4 \\ \hline \end{array}$ **7.** $\begin{array}{r} 15 \\ \times\,8 \\ \hline \end{array}$ **8.** $\begin{array}{r} 18 \\ \times\,7 \\ \hline \end{array}$ **9.** $\begin{array}{r} 33 \\ \times\,6 \\ \hline \end{array}$ **10.** $\begin{array}{r} 54 \\ \times\,7 \\ \hline \end{array}$

11. $\begin{array}{r} 45 \\ \times\,3 \\ \hline \end{array}$ **12.** $\begin{array}{r} 52 \\ \times\,6 \\ \hline \end{array}$ **13.** $\begin{array}{r} 63 \\ \times\,4 \\ \hline \end{array}$ **14.** $\begin{array}{r} 72 \\ \times\,5 \\ \hline \end{array}$ **15.** $\begin{array}{r} 93 \\ \times\,4 \\ \hline \end{array}$

Whole Numbers: Multiplication

REMEMBER?
4
7 9
$\times$ 5
? 9 5

1. $\begin{array}{r} 97 \\ \times\ 3 \\ \hline \end{array}$ **2.** $\begin{array}{r} 56 \\ \times\ 8 \\ \hline \end{array}$ **3.** $\begin{array}{r} 75 \\ \times\ 2 \\ \hline \end{array}$ **4.** $\begin{array}{r} 68 \\ \times\ 2 \\ \hline \end{array}$

5. $\begin{array}{r} 45 \\ \times\ 7 \\ \hline \end{array}$ **6.** $\begin{array}{r} 79 \\ \times\ 5 \\ \hline \end{array}$ **7.** $\begin{array}{r} 52 \\ \times\ 7 \\ \hline \end{array}$ **8.** $\begin{array}{r} 67 \\ \times\ 3 \\ \hline \end{array}$ **9.** $\begin{array}{r} 94 \\ \times\ 5 \\ \hline \end{array}$

10. $\begin{array}{r} 18 \\ \times\ 6 \\ \hline \end{array}$ **11.** $\begin{array}{r} 96 \\ \times\ 4 \\ \hline \end{array}$ **12.** $\begin{array}{r} 55 \\ \times\ 5 \\ \hline \end{array}$ **13.** $\begin{array}{r} 27 \\ \times\ 9 \\ \hline \end{array}$ **14.** $\begin{array}{r} 98 \\ \times\ 8 \\ \hline \end{array}$

15. $\begin{array}{r} 23 \\ \times\ 7 \\ \hline \end{array}$ **16.** $\begin{array}{r} 54 \\ \times\ 8 \\ \hline \end{array}$ **17.** $\begin{array}{r} 36 \\ \times\ 3 \\ \hline \end{array}$ **18.** $\begin{array}{r} 99 \\ \times\ 4 \\ \hline \end{array}$ **19.** $\begin{array}{r} 25 \\ \times\ 6 \\ \hline \end{array}$

20. $\begin{array}{r} 98 \\ \times\ 4 \\ \hline \end{array}$ **21.** $\begin{array}{r} 57 \\ \times\ 7 \\ \hline \end{array}$ **22.** $\begin{array}{r} 26 \\ \times\ 6 \\ \hline \end{array}$ **23.** $\begin{array}{r} 69 \\ \times\ 3 \\ \hline \end{array}$ **24.** $\begin{array}{r} 78 \\ \times\ 4 \\ \hline \end{array}$

25. $\begin{array}{r} 53 \\ \times\ 6 \\ \hline \end{array}$ **26.** $\begin{array}{r} 68 \\ \times\ 4 \\ \hline \end{array}$ **27.** $\begin{array}{r} 95 \\ \times\ 5 \\ \hline \end{array}$ **28.** $\begin{array}{r} 28 \\ \times\ 7 \\ \hline \end{array}$ **29.** $\begin{array}{r} 97 \\ \times\ 3 \\ \hline \end{array}$

Whole Numbers: Multiplication

1. $\begin{array}{r} 39 \\ \times\ 6 \\ \hline \end{array}$
2. $\begin{array}{r} 48 \\ \times\ 7 \\ \hline \end{array}$
3. $\begin{array}{r} 89 \\ \times\ 5 \\ \hline \end{array}$
4. $\begin{array}{r} 58 \\ \times\ 7 \\ \hline \end{array}$
5. $\begin{array}{r} 76 \\ \times\ 7 \\ \hline \end{array}$

6. $\begin{array}{r} 44 \\ \times\ 7 \\ \hline \end{array}$
7. $\begin{array}{r} 67 \\ \times\ 3 \\ \hline \end{array}$
8. $\begin{array}{r} 58 \\ \times\ 3 \\ \hline \end{array}$
9. $\begin{array}{r} 89 \\ \times\ 8 \\ \hline \end{array}$
10. $\begin{array}{r} 85 \\ \times\ 4 \\ \hline \end{array}$

11. $\begin{array}{r} 58 \\ \times\ 8 \\ \hline \end{array}$
12. $\begin{array}{r} 27 \\ \times\ 9 \\ \hline \end{array}$
13. $\begin{array}{r} 36 \\ \times\ 4 \\ \hline \end{array}$
14. $\begin{array}{r} 66 \\ \times\ 6 \\ \hline \end{array}$
15. $\begin{array}{r} 84 \\ \times\ 3 \\ \hline \end{array}$

16. $\begin{array}{r} 72 \\ \times\ 9 \\ \hline \end{array}$
17. $\begin{array}{r} 98 \\ \times\ 9 \\ \hline \end{array}$
18. $\begin{array}{r} 74 \\ \times\ 5 \\ \hline \end{array}$
19. $\begin{array}{r} 36 \\ \times\ 8 \\ \hline \end{array}$
20. $\begin{array}{r} 76 \\ \times\ 8 \\ \hline \end{array}$

21. $\begin{array}{r} 59 \\ \times\ 4 \\ \hline \end{array}$
22. $\begin{array}{r} 77 \\ \times\ 7 \\ \hline \end{array}$
23. $\begin{array}{r} 48 \\ \times\ 6 \\ \hline \end{array}$
24. $\begin{array}{r} 53 \\ \times\ 7 \\ \hline \end{array}$
25. $\begin{array}{r} 49 \\ \times\ 4 \\ \hline \end{array}$

26. $\begin{array}{r} 27 \\ \times\ 6 \\ \hline \end{array}$
27. $\begin{array}{r} 57 \\ \times\ 7 \\ \hline \end{array}$
28. $\begin{array}{r} 43 \\ \times\ 8 \\ \hline \end{array}$
29. $\begin{array}{r} 65 \\ \times\ 6 \\ \hline \end{array}$
30. $\begin{array}{r} 87 \\ \times\ 9 \\ \hline \end{array}$

Whole Numbers: Multiplication

REMEMBER?

$$522 \quad 522 \quad 522$$
$$\times\,4 \quad \times\,4 \quad \times\,4$$

A

1. 712
$\times\,3$

2. 512
$\times\,4$

3. 611
$\times\,8$

4. 421
$\times\,4$

5. 263
$\times\,2$

6. 281
$\times\,3$

7. 171
$\times\,5$

8. 493
$\times\,2$

9. 227
$\times\,3$

10. 216
$\times\,4$

11. 119
$\times\,5$

12. 127
$\times\,3$

13. 219
$\times\,4$

- -

B

1. 413
$\times\,3$

2. 522
$\times\,4$

3. 911
$\times\,9$

4. 412
$\times\,4$

5. 821
$\times\,3$

6. 271
$\times\,3$

7. 292
$\times\,2$

8. 181
$\times\,5$

9. 481
$\times\,2$

10. 191
$\times\,4$

11. 126
$\times\,3$

12. 228
$\times\,3$

13. 118
$\times\,5$

14. 226
$\times\,3$

15. 217
$\times\,4$

Whole Numbers: Multiplication

REMEMBER?

$$\begin{array}{r} 3 \\ 168 \\ \times 4 \\ \hline \end{array} \quad \begin{array}{r} 2\;3 \\ 168 \\ \times 4 \\ \hline \end{array} \quad \begin{array}{r} 2\;3 \\ 168 \\ \times 4 \\ \hline \end{array}$$

A

1. 154×3
2. 118×8
3. 237×4

4. 149×6
5. 238×4
6. 157×5
7. 466×2
8. 169×4

9. 387×2
10. 133×7
11. 285×3
12. 136×5
13. 486×2

B

1. 123×8
2. 158×3
3. 169×4
4. 119×8
5. 157×5

6. 176×5
7. 228×4
8. 133×6
9. 227×4
10. 182×3

11. 359×2
12. 286×3
13. 498×2
14. 186×4
15. 455×2

Whole Numbers: Multiplication

REMEMBER?
3 2
2 6 4
× 6
?,? 8 4

A

1. 464
× 3

2. 357
× 3

3. 557
× 4

4. 324
× 9

5. 428
× 6

6. 532
× 8

7. 297
× 6

8. 448
× 4

9. 747
× 3

10. 435
× 4

11. 324
× 5

12. 275
× 6

13. 536
× 7

14. 618
× 7

B

1. 358
× 5

2. 469
× 3

3. 468
× 5

4. 558
× 4

5. 264
× 6

6. 486
× 5

7. 359
× 6

8. 676
× 7

9. 359
× 4

10. 568
× 4

11. 375
× 4

12. 443
× 6

13. 734
× 7

14. 837
× 6

15. 555
× 8

Whole Numbers: Multiplication

A

REMEMBER?
3 2
2,1 7 4
× 5
? ?,? 7 0

1. 2,498
× 2

2. 1,138
× 6

3. 2,239
× 4

4. 3,708
× 9

5. 1,268
× 4

6. 1,105
× 8

7. 2,248
× 4

8. 1,109
× 6

9. 2,376
× 2

10. 1,168
× 6

11. 3,047
× 3

- -

B

1. 1,258
× 3

2. 1,267
× 2

3. 2,169
× 4

4. 3,398
× 2

5. 1,136
× 5

6. 2,193
× 4

7. 1,118
× 8

8. 1,136
× 7

9. 2,149
× 3

10. 1,358
× 2

11. 2,188
× 4

12. 1,154
× 6

Whole Numbers: Multiplication

A

1. 1,139
   $\times\ 5$

2. 1,238
   $\times\ 6$

3. 1,426
   $\times\ 5$

4. 2,388
   $\times\ 4$

5. 4,306
   $\times\ 7$

6. 4,113
   $\times\ 6$

7. 3,467
   $\times\ 8$

8. 4,405
   $\times\ 3$

9. 3,452
   $\times\ 6$

10. 1,384
    $\times\ 9$

11. 4,453
    $\times\ 5$

12. 5,411
    $\times\ 4$

B

1. 2,187
   $\times\ 4$

2. 1,060
   $\times\ 9$

3. 2,716
   $\times\ 3$

4. 2,473
   $\times\ 4$

5. 3,738
   $\times\ 9$

6. 3,854
   $\times\ 7$

7. 5,862
   $\times\ 6$

8. 4,483
   $\times\ 5$

9. 2,158
   $\times\ 6$

10. 4,059
    $\times\ 8$

11. 7,185
    $\times\ 9$

12. 2,058
    $\times\ 8$

Name _____   Date _____

Whole Numbers: Multiplication

SKILL 1

1.   8
    $\times$ 6

2.   7
    $\times$ 4

3.   5
    $\times$ 9

4.   6
    $\times$ 3

5.   9
    $\times$ 9

SKILL 2

6.   34
    $\times$ 2

7.   23
    $\times$ 3

8. 322
    $\times$ 3

9. 110
    $\times$ 7

10. 312
    $\times$ 3

SKILL 3

11. 17
    $\times$ 5

12. 16
    $\times$ 6

13. 223
    $\times$ 4

14. 336
    $\times$ 2

15. 116
    $\times$ 5

SKILL 4

16. 37
    $\times$ 6

17. 67
    $\times$ 7

18. 54
    $\times$ 8

19. 76
    $\times$ 6

20. 79
    $\times$ 9

SKILL 5

21. 644
    $\times$ 6

22. 774
    $\times$ 3

23. 479
    $\times$ 5

24. 543
    $\times$ 7

25. 658
    $\times$ 4

26. 4,559
    $\times$ 5

27. 8,678
    $\times$ 3

28. 6,408
    $\times$ 6

29. 2,355
    $\times$ 5

Name _____   Date _____

Whole Numbers: Multiplication

SKILL 6 • Practice

Page 1

REMEMBER?
80   80
× 10   × 10

A

1. 20
  × 30

2. 30
  × 30

3. 20
  × 40

4. 10
  × 50

5. 10
  × 90

6. 80
  × 10

7. 10
  × 40

8. 70
  × 10

9. 60
  × 10

10. 10
  × 90

11. 20
  × 10

12. 40
  × 20

13. 50
  × 10

14. 10
  × 70

- -

B

1. 10
  × 30

2. 90
  × 10

3. 40
  × 20

4. 70
  × 10

5. 10
  × 60

6. 20
  × 40

7. 30
  × 30

8. 50
  × 10

9. 10
  × 40

10. 30
  × 20

11. 20
  × 20

12. 40
  × 10

13. 10
  × 70

14. 30
  × 10

15. 10
  × 80

Copyright © Houghton Mifflin Company. All rights reserved.

Whole Numbers: Multiplication • Skill

Whole Numbers: Multiplication

REMEMBER?

$$\begin{array}{r} 40 \\ \times\, 30 \\ \hline \end{array} \qquad \begin{array}{r} 40 \\ \times\, 30 \\ \hline \end{array}$$

A

1. $\begin{array}{r} 90 \\ \times\, 60 \\ \hline \end{array}$	2. $\begin{array}{r} 80 \\ \times\, 30 \\ \hline \end{array}$	3. $\begin{array}{r} 40 \\ \times\, 60 \\ \hline \end{array}$	4. $\begin{array}{r} 50 \\ \times\, 70 \\ \hline \end{array}$

5. $\begin{array}{r} 60 \\ \times\, 30 \\ \hline \end{array}$	6. $\begin{array}{r} 50 \\ \times\, 90 \\ \hline \end{array}$	7. $\begin{array}{r} 60 \\ \times\, 90 \\ \hline \end{array}$	8. $\begin{array}{r} 70 \\ \times\, 50 \\ \hline \end{array}$	9. $\begin{array}{r} 40 \\ \times\, 90 \\ \hline \end{array}$

10. $\begin{array}{r} 30 \\ \times\, 50 \\ \hline \end{array}$	11. $\begin{array}{r} 90 \\ \times\, 70 \\ \hline \end{array}$	12. $\begin{array}{r} 80 \\ \times\, 60 \\ \hline \end{array}$	13. $\begin{array}{r} 40 \\ \times\, 50 \\ \hline \end{array}$	14. $\begin{array}{r} 50 \\ \times\, 50 \\ \hline \end{array}$

- -

B

1. $\begin{array}{r} 70 \\ \times\, 30 \\ \hline \end{array}$	2. $\begin{array}{r} 80 \\ \times\, 50 \\ \hline \end{array}$	3. $\begin{array}{r} 80 \\ \times\, 40 \\ \hline \end{array}$	4. $\begin{array}{r} 50 \\ \times\, 30 \\ \hline \end{array}$	5. $\begin{array}{r} 90 \\ \times\, 90 \\ \hline \end{array}$

6. $\begin{array}{r} 40 \\ \times\, 80 \\ \hline \end{array}$	7. $\begin{array}{r} 80 \\ \times\, 80 \\ \hline \end{array}$	8. $\begin{array}{r} 40 \\ \times\, 90 \\ \hline \end{array}$	9. $\begin{array}{r} 60 \\ \times\, 70 \\ \hline \end{array}$	10. $\begin{array}{r} 30 \\ \times\, 90 \\ \hline \end{array}$

11. $\begin{array}{r} 60 \\ \times\, 80 \\ \hline \end{array}$	12. $\begin{array}{r} 70 \\ \times\, 40 \\ \hline \end{array}$	13. $\begin{array}{r} 90 \\ \times\, 50 \\ \hline \end{array}$	14. $\begin{array}{r} 80 \\ \times\, 90 \\ \hline \end{array}$	15. $\begin{array}{r} 50 \\ \times\, 60 \\ \hline \end{array}$

Whole Numbers: Multiplication

REMEMBER?		
43	43	40
× 20	× 20	× 20

A

1. 33
  × 10

2. 37
  × 10

3. 11
  × 50

4. 75
  × 10

5. 32
  × 10

6. 24
  × 20

7. 44
  × 20

8. 73
  × 10

9. 32
  × 30

10. 65
  × 10

11. 42
  × 20

12. 34
  × 20

13. 31
  × 20

B

1. 43
  × 20

2. 82
  × 10

3. 44
  × 10

4. 93
  × 10

5. 33
  × 30

6. 44
  × 20

7. 68
  × 10

8. 23
  × 20

9. 12
  × 40

10. 22
  × 30

11. 54
  × 10

12. 78
  × 10

13. 42
  × 20

14. 14
  × 20

15. 89
  × 10

Name _____   Date _____

Whole Numbers:
Multiplication

SKILL 6 • Practice
Page 4

REMEMBER?
3
3 6
× 5 0
?,? 0 0

1. 38
× 50

2. 95
× 80

3. 29
× 60

4. 33
× 80

5. 37
× 20

6. 27
× 40

7. 28
× 90

8. 73
× 70

9. 54
× 60

10. 18
× 40

11. 15
× 70

12. 58
× 40

13. 48
× 30

14. 96
× 90

15. 33
× 80

16. 58
× 40

17. 95
× 80

18. 37
× 50

19. 34
× 60

20. 49
× 40

21. 84
× 70

22. 38
× 60

23. 42
× 80

24. 24
× 30

25. 36
× 70

26. 19
× 90

27. 62
× 50

28. 45
× 20

29. 29
× 60

Whole Numbers: Multiplication • Skill 6

Copyright © Houghton Mifflin Company. All rights reserved.

Whole Numbers: Multiplication

A

1. $\begin{array}{r} 355 \\ \times\ 20 \\ \hline \end{array}$	2. $\begin{array}{r} 243 \\ \times\ 40 \\ \hline \end{array}$	3. $\begin{array}{r} 136 \\ \times\ 30 \\ \hline \end{array}$	4. $\begin{array}{r} 478 \\ \times\ 20 \\ \hline \end{array}$
5. $\begin{array}{r} 343 \\ \times\ 70 \\ \hline \end{array}$	6. $\begin{array}{r} 836 \\ \times\ 30 \\ \hline \end{array}$	7. $\begin{array}{r} 964 \\ \times\ 30 \\ \hline \end{array}$	8. $\begin{array}{r} 838 \\ \times\ 40 \\ \hline \end{array}$
9. $\begin{array}{r} 468 \\ \times\ 30 \\ \hline \end{array}$	10. $\begin{array}{r} 854 \\ \times\ 30 \\ \hline \end{array}$	11. $\begin{array}{r} 838 \\ \times\ 40 \\ \hline \end{array}$	12. $\begin{array}{r} 395 \\ \times\ 50 \\ \hline \end{array}$

B

1. $\begin{array}{r} 175 \\ \times\ 40 \\ \hline \end{array}$	2. $\begin{array}{r} 236 \\ \times\ 30 \\ \hline \end{array}$	3. $\begin{array}{r} 367 \\ \times\ 20 \\ \hline \end{array}$	4. $\begin{array}{r} 182 \\ \times\ 50 \\ \hline \end{array}$
5. $\begin{array}{r} 549 \\ \times\ 50 \\ \hline \end{array}$	6. $\begin{array}{r} 708 \\ \times\ 50 \\ \hline \end{array}$	7. $\begin{array}{r} 418 \\ \times\ 60 \\ \hline \end{array}$	8. $\begin{array}{r} 326 \\ \times\ 80 \\ \hline \end{array}$
9. $\begin{array}{r} 419 \\ \times\ 70 \\ \hline \end{array}$	10. $\begin{array}{r} 754 \\ \times\ 40 \\ \hline \end{array}$	11. $\begin{array}{r} 762 \\ \times\ 50 \\ \hline \end{array}$	12. $\begin{array}{r} 629 \\ \times\ 70 \\ \hline \end{array}$

Whole Numbers: Multiplication

A

1. 2,364 $\times\ 40$	**2.** 1,645 $\times\ 30$	**3.** 1,255 $\times\ 40$	**4.** 1,968 $\times\ 20$
5. 6,732 $\times\ 30$	**6.** 3,673 $\times\ 20$	**7.** 4,623 $\times\ 40$	**8.** 5,702 $\times\ 50$
9. 2,658 $\times\ 40$	**10.** 3,227 $\times\ 80$	**11.** 2,905 $\times\ 90$	**12.** 3,724 $\times\ 60$

- -

B

1. 1,278 $\times\ 60$	**2.** 1,895 $\times\ 20$	**3.** 3,465 $\times\ 20$	**4.** 2,565 $\times\ 30$
5. 3,742 $\times\ 30$	**6.** 1,892 $\times\ 40$	**7.** 3,245 $\times\ 30$	**8.** 2,038 $\times\ 40$
9. 4,256 $\times\ 70$	**10.** 2,658 $\times\ 40$	**11.** 3,742 $\times\ 80$	**12.** 2,927 $\times\ 50$

Whole Numbers:
Multiplication

REMEMBER?
234
× 100
??,?00

A

1. 321
    × 300

2. 231
    × 200

3. 211
    × 400

4. 434
    × 200

5. 122
    × 400

6. 898
    × 100

7. 221
    × 300

8. 243
    × 200

9. 222
    × 400

10. 764
    × 100

11. 213
    × 300

B

1. 782
    × 100

2. 330
    × 300

3. 202
    × 200

4. 212
    × 400

5. 332
    × 300

6. 404
    × 200

7. 121
    × 400

8. 936
    × 100

9. 240
    × 200

10. 201
    × 400

11. 545
    × 100

12. 103
    × 300

Whole Numbers: Multiplication

REMEMBER?
$\begin{array}{r} 1\ 2 \\ 3\ 4\ 7 \\ \times\ 3\ 0\ 0 \end{array}$

A

1. $\begin{array}{r} 465 \\ \times\ 200 \end{array}$
2. $\begin{array}{r} 157 \\ \times\ 500 \end{array}$
3. $\begin{array}{r} 496 \\ \times\ 200 \end{array}$

4. $\begin{array}{r} 278 \\ \times\ 300 \end{array}$
5. $\begin{array}{r} 965 \\ \times\ 300 \end{array}$
6. $\begin{array}{r} 272 \\ \times\ 700 \end{array}$
7. $\begin{array}{r} 509 \\ \times\ 700 \end{array}$

8. $\begin{array}{r} 379 \\ \times\ 400 \end{array}$
9. $\begin{array}{r} 569 \\ \times\ 400 \end{array}$
10. $\begin{array}{r} 182 \\ \times\ 600 \end{array}$
11. $\begin{array}{r} 367 \\ \times\ 500 \end{array}$

B

1. $\begin{array}{r} 358 \\ \times\ 200 \end{array}$
2. $\begin{array}{r} 148 \\ \times\ 500 \end{array}$
3. $\begin{array}{r} 267 \\ \times\ 200 \end{array}$
4. $\begin{array}{r} 249 \\ \times\ 300 \end{array}$

5. $\begin{array}{r} 163 \\ \times\ 600 \end{array}$
6. $\begin{array}{r} 328 \\ \times\ 400 \end{array}$
7. $\begin{array}{r} 937 \\ \times\ 300 \end{array}$
8. $\begin{array}{r} 268 \\ \times\ 800 \end{array}$

9. $\begin{array}{r} 433 \\ \times\ 900 \end{array}$
10. $\begin{array}{r} 968 \\ \times\ 300 \end{array}$
11. $\begin{array}{r} 578 \\ \times\ 500 \end{array}$
12. $\begin{array}{r} 482 \\ \times\ 600 \end{array}$

Whole Numbers: Multiplication

REMEMBER?

$$\begin{array}{r} 1\ 1\ 1 \\ 2,5\,6\,5 \\ \times\ 3\,0\,0 \\ \hline \end{array}$$

A

1. $\begin{array}{r} 2,278 \\ \times\ 400 \\ \hline \end{array}$

2. $\begin{array}{r} 3,567 \\ \times\ 200 \\ \hline \end{array}$

3. $\begin{array}{r} 2,439 \\ \times\ 300 \\ \hline \end{array}$

4. $\begin{array}{r} 2,239 \\ \times\ 400 \\ \hline \end{array}$

5. $\begin{array}{r} 3,916 \\ \times\ 400 \\ \hline \end{array}$

6. $\begin{array}{r} 2,602 \\ \times\ 500 \\ \hline \end{array}$

7. $\begin{array}{r} 2,046 \\ \times\ 600 \\ \hline \end{array}$

8. $\begin{array}{r} 6,742 \\ \times\ 300 \\ \hline \end{array}$

9. $\begin{array}{r} 4,867 \\ \times\ 400 \\ \hline \end{array}$

10. $\begin{array}{r} 2,077 \\ \times\ 600 \\ \hline \end{array}$

11. $\begin{array}{r} 5,985 \\ \times\ 700 \\ \hline \end{array}$

B

1. $\begin{array}{r} 4,786 \\ \times\ 200 \\ \hline \end{array}$

2. $\begin{array}{r} 1,289 \\ \times\ 400 \\ \hline \end{array}$

3. $\begin{array}{r} 2,269 \\ \times\ 400 \\ \hline \end{array}$

4. $\begin{array}{r} 1,536 \\ \times\ 300 \\ \hline \end{array}$

5. $\begin{array}{r} 3,658 \\ \times\ 200 \\ \hline \end{array}$

6. $\begin{array}{r} 4,562 \\ \times\ 300 \\ \hline \end{array}$

7. $\begin{array}{r} 5,340 \\ \times\ 500 \\ \hline \end{array}$

8. $\begin{array}{r} 6,307 \\ \times\ 400 \\ \hline \end{array}$

9. $\begin{array}{r} 2,157 \\ \times\ 600 \\ \hline \end{array}$

10. $\begin{array}{r} 3,066 \\ \times\ 500 \\ \hline \end{array}$

11. $\begin{array}{r} 5,224 \\ \times\ 600 \\ \hline \end{array}$

12. $\begin{array}{r} 4,538 \\ \times\ 300 \\ \hline \end{array}$

Name _____   Date _____

Whole Numbers: Multiplication

SKILL 8 • Practice
Page 1

REMEMBER?
1,232
× 3,000
000

A

1. 2,232
× 3,000

2. 1,212
× 4,000

3. 1,011
× 5,000

4. 3,431
× 2,000

5. 1,322
× 3,000

6. 3,124
× 2,000

7. 2,132
× 3,000

8. 4,023
× 2,000

- -

B

1. 1,210
× 4,000

2. 2,324
× 2,000

3. 2,230
× 3,000

4. 1,042
× 1,000

5. 1,011
× 5,000

6. 1,202
× 4,000

7. 1,233
× 3,000

8. 3,044
× 2,000

9. 3,133
× 3,000

Copyright © Houghton Mifflin Company. All rights reserved.

Whole Numbers: Multiplication • Skill 8

Name _____   Date _____

Whole Numbers: Multiplication

REMEMBER?

```
  1  1  1
  5, 6 7 8
× 2, 0 0 0
```

A

1. 4,364
   × 3,000

2. 8,234
   × 5,000

3. 9,486
   × 3,000

4. 4,273
   × 4,000

5. 6,303
   × 5,000

6. 3,043
   × 4,000

7. 9,861
   × 3,000

8. 4,114
   × 6,000

B

1. 7,638
   × 3,000

2. 6,875
   × 2,000

3. 5,487
   × 4,000

4. 1,437
   × 9,000

5. 7,345
   × 5,000

6. 3,529
   × 2,000

7. 4,305
   × 4,000

8. 6,073
   × 6,000

9. 3,545
   × 3,000

Whole Numbers: Multiplication

REMEMBER?

$$
\begin{array}{r}
{\scriptstyle 2\ 1\ 1\ 2} \\
1\,6,4\,3\,5 \\
\times\ 4,0\,0\,0 \\
\hline
\end{array}
$$

A

1. $\begin{array}{r} 19{,}763 \\ \times\ 4{,}000 \\ \hline \end{array}$

2. $\begin{array}{r} 43{,}216 \\ \times\ 5{,}000 \\ \hline \end{array}$

3. $\begin{array}{r} 33{,}201 \\ \times\ 6{,}000 \\ \hline \end{array}$

4. $\begin{array}{r} 52{,}136 \\ \times\ 2{,}000 \\ \hline \end{array}$

5. $\begin{array}{r} 73{,}041 \\ \times\ 3{,}000 \\ \hline \end{array}$

6. $\begin{array}{r} 24{,}564 \\ \times\ 5{,}000 \\ \hline \end{array}$

7. $\begin{array}{r} 18{,}773 \\ \times\ 6{,}000 \\ \hline \end{array}$

8. $\begin{array}{r} 44{,}302 \\ \times\ 4{,}000 \\ \hline \end{array}$

B

1. $\begin{array}{r} 25{,}436 \\ \times\ 3{,}000 \\ \hline \end{array}$

2. $\begin{array}{r} 17{,}542 \\ \times\ 4{,}000 \\ \hline \end{array}$

3. $\begin{array}{r} 46{,}318 \\ \times\ 5{,}000 \\ \hline \end{array}$

4. $\begin{array}{r} 36{,}403 \\ \times\ 6{,}000 \\ \hline \end{array}$

5. $\begin{array}{r} 56{,}403 \\ \times\ 2{,}000 \\ \hline \end{array}$

6. $\begin{array}{r} 66{,}410 \\ \times\ 7{,}000 \\ \hline \end{array}$

7. $\begin{array}{r} 72{,}063 \\ \times\ 3{,}000 \\ \hline \end{array}$

8. $\begin{array}{r} 26{,}723 \\ \times\ 5{,}000 \\ \hline \end{array}$

9. $\begin{array}{r} 15{,}473 \\ \times\ 6{,}000 \\ \hline \end{array}$

Whole Numbers: Multiplication

REMEMBER?
22   22
× 44   × 44

A

1. 15
× 11

2. 23
× 13

3. 21
× 34

4. 42
× 22

5. 33
× 22

6. 31
× 33

7. 12
× 23

8. 18
× 11

9. 33
× 11

B

1. 22
× 44

2. 33
× 33

3. 19
× 11

4. 42
× 22

5. 44
× 21

6. 23
× 31

7. 24
× 12

8. 31
× 22

9. 14
× 11

10. 13
× 22

Whole Numbers: Multiplication

REMEMBER?
77   77
× 17   × 17

A

1. 86
   × 18

2. 47
   × 26

3. 39
   × 24

4. 48
   × 25

5. 77
   × 17

6. 28
   × 26

7. 37
   × 28

8. 45
   × 29

9. 96
   × 19

- -

B

1. 46
   × 29

2. 35
   × 28

3. 58
   × 16

4. 49
   × 25

5. 67
   × 16

6. 27
   × 19

7. 46
   × 26

8. 27
   × 28

9. 88
   × 18

10. 36
   × 26

Whole Numbers: Multiplication

A

1. $\begin{array}{r} 58 \\ \times\ 27 \\ \hline \end{array}$	2. $\begin{array}{r} 39 \\ \times\ 75 \\ \hline \end{array}$	3. $\begin{array}{r} 56 \\ \times\ 34 \\ \hline \end{array}$	4. $\begin{array}{r} 46 \\ \times\ 45 \\ \hline \end{array}$	5. $\begin{array}{r} 49 \\ \times\ 36 \\ \hline \end{array}$
6. $\begin{array}{r} 47 \\ \times\ 39 \\ \hline \end{array}$	7. $\begin{array}{r} 77 \\ \times\ 33 \\ \hline \end{array}$	8. $\begin{array}{r} 94 \\ \times\ 37 \\ \hline \end{array}$	9. $\begin{array}{r} 82 \\ \times\ 65 \\ \hline \end{array}$	10. $\begin{array}{r} 62 \\ \times\ 37 \\ \hline \end{array}$

- -

B

1. $\begin{array}{r} 97 \\ \times\ 23 \\ \hline \end{array}$	2. $\begin{array}{r} 65 \\ \times\ 36 \\ \hline \end{array}$	3. $\begin{array}{r} 58 \\ \times\ 34 \\ \hline \end{array}$	4. $\begin{array}{r} 23 \\ \times\ 99 \\ \hline \end{array}$	5. $\begin{array}{r} 68 \\ \times\ 28 \\ \hline \end{array}$
6. $\begin{array}{r} 38 \\ \times\ 43 \\ \hline \end{array}$	7. $\begin{array}{r} 96 \\ \times\ 47 \\ \hline \end{array}$	8. $\begin{array}{r} 59 \\ \times\ 95 \\ \hline \end{array}$	9. $\begin{array}{r} 77 \\ \times\ 27 \\ \hline \end{array}$	10. $\begin{array}{r} 94 \\ \times\ 35 \\ \hline \end{array}$

Whole Numbers: Multiplication

1. $\begin{array}{r} 16 \\ \times\, 11 \\ \hline \end{array}$ 2. $\begin{array}{r} 24 \\ \times\, 12 \\ \hline \end{array}$ 3. $\begin{array}{r} 40 \\ \times\, 23 \\ \hline \end{array}$ 4. $\begin{array}{r} 21 \\ \times\, 35 \\ \hline \end{array}$ 5. $\begin{array}{r} 34 \\ \times\, 31 \\ \hline \end{array}$

6. $\begin{array}{r} 35 \\ \times\, 29 \\ \hline \end{array}$ 7. $\begin{array}{r} 87 \\ \times\, 19 \\ \hline \end{array}$ 8. $\begin{array}{r} 47 \\ \times\, 25 \\ \hline \end{array}$ 9. $\begin{array}{r} 38 \\ \times\, 24 \\ \hline \end{array}$ 10. $\begin{array}{r} 29 \\ \times\, 36 \\ \hline \end{array}$

11. $\begin{array}{r} 98 \\ \times\, 22 \\ \hline \end{array}$ 12. $\begin{array}{r} 66 \\ \times\, 37 \\ \hline \end{array}$ 13. $\begin{array}{r} 59 \\ \times\, 35 \\ \hline \end{array}$ 14. $\begin{array}{r} 24 \\ \times\, 88 \\ \hline \end{array}$ 15. $\begin{array}{r} 69 \\ \times\, 29 \\ \hline \end{array}$

16. $\begin{array}{r} 48 \\ \times\, 44 \\ \hline \end{array}$ 17. $\begin{array}{r} 86 \\ \times\, 57 \\ \hline \end{array}$ 18. $\begin{array}{r} 62 \\ \times\, 96 \\ \hline \end{array}$ 19. $\begin{array}{r} 78 \\ \times\, 36 \\ \hline \end{array}$ 20. $\begin{array}{r} 95 \\ \times\, 34 \\ \hline \end{array}$

Name _____ Date _____

Whole Numbers: Multiplication

REMEMBER?
123   123
× 23   × 23

A

1. 323
   × 12

2. 221
   × 34

3. 342
   × 22

4. 233
   × 33

5. 312
   × 23

6. 918
   × 11

7. 433
   × 21

8. 242
   × 12

- -

B

1. 122
   × 44

2. 223
   × 33

3. 519
   × 11

4. 432
   × 22

5. 244
   × 21

6. 323
   × 31

7. 224
   × 12

8. 331
   × 23

9. 414
   × 21

10. 413
    × 12

Whole Numbers: Multiplication

REMEMBER?
234   234
× 24   × 24

A

1. $\begin{array}{r} 444 \\ \times\ 28 \\ \hline \end{array}$ 2. $\begin{array}{r} 872 \\ \times\ 19 \\ \hline \end{array}$ 3. $\begin{array}{r} 709 \\ \times\ 16 \\ \hline \end{array}$

4. $\begin{array}{r} 414 \\ \times\ 29 \\ \hline \end{array}$ 5. $\begin{array}{r} 323 \\ \times\ 27 \\ \hline \end{array}$ 6. $\begin{array}{r} 506 \\ \times\ 17 \\ \hline \end{array}$ 7. $\begin{array}{r} 232 \\ \times\ 37 \\ \hline \end{array}$ 8. $\begin{array}{r} 494 \\ \times\ 15 \\ \hline \end{array}$

B

1. $\begin{array}{r} 234 \\ \times\ 26 \\ \hline \end{array}$ 2. $\begin{array}{r} 808 \\ \times\ 17 \\ \hline \end{array}$ 3. $\begin{array}{r} 344 \\ \times\ 29 \\ \hline \end{array}$ 4. $\begin{array}{r} 224 \\ \times\ 28 \\ \hline \end{array}$ 5. $\begin{array}{r} 233 \\ \times\ 36 \\ \hline \end{array}$

6. $\begin{array}{r} 608 \\ \times\ 18 \\ \hline \end{array}$ 7. $\begin{array}{r} 443 \\ \times\ 24 \\ \hline \end{array}$ 8. $\begin{array}{r} 399 \\ \times\ 14 \\ \hline \end{array}$ 9. $\begin{array}{r} 494 \\ \times\ 18 \\ \hline \end{array}$ 10. $\begin{array}{r} 444 \\ \times\ 29 \\ \hline \end{array}$

Whole Numbers: Multiplication

REMEMBER?
849   849
× 33   × 33

1. 153
   × 58

2. 494
   × 26

3. 209
   × 35

4. 598
   × 18

5. 169
   × 45

6. 103
   × 49

7. 598
   × 16

8. 258
   × 25

9. 302
   × 28

10. 295
   × 37

11. 368
   × 24

12. 273
   × 34

13. 183
   × 59

14. 260
   × 38

15. 153
   × 78

16. 496
   × 27

17. 906
   × 15

18. 839
   × 13

Whole Numbers: Multiplication

REMEMBER?
2,233
× 32
?,?66

A

1. 1,341
    × 21

2. 2,323
    × 33

3. 2,434
    × 22

4. 3,354
    × 18

5. 2,342
    × 29

6. 2,526
    × 17

7. 2,133
    × 38

- -

B

1. 2,134
    × 20

2. 1,432
    × 22

3. 3,322
    × 31

4. 3,323
    × 23

5. 2,463
    × 18

6. 2,433
    × 26

7. 2,768
    × 16

8. 2,144
    × 29

Whole Numbers: Multiplication

A

1. 4,736
   $\times\ 36$

2. 8,533
   $\times\ 13$

3. 2,466
   $\times\ 30$

4. 9,318
   $\times\ 24$

5. 4,270
   $\times\ 16$

6. 1,784
   $\times\ 92$

7. 1,376
   $\times\ 54$

8. 2,473
   $\times\ 58$

- -

B

1. 9,249
   $\times\ 25$

2. 1,386
   $\times\ 99$

3. 1,829
   $\times\ 69$

4. 2,545
   $\times\ 76$

5. 1,230
   $\times\ 95$

6. 2,372
   $\times\ 90$

7. 1,488
   $\times\ 73$

8. 4,066
   $\times\ 73$

Whole Numbers: Multiplication

REMEMBER?
326   326
$\times$ 34 $\times$ 34

A

1. $\begin{array}{r} 2,344 \\ \times\ 46 \\ \hline \end{array}$

2. $\begin{array}{r} 334 \\ \times\ 98 \\ \hline \end{array}$

3. $\begin{array}{r} 1,124 \\ \times\ 48 \\ \hline \end{array}$

4. $\begin{array}{r} 318 \\ \times\ 68 \\ \hline \end{array}$

5. $\begin{array}{r} 1,419 \\ \times\ 88 \\ \hline \end{array}$

6. $\begin{array}{r} 3,634 \\ \times\ 28 \\ \hline \end{array}$

7. $\begin{array}{r} 776 \\ \times\ 92 \\ \hline \end{array}$

B

1. $\begin{array}{r} 647 \\ \times\ 43 \\ \hline \end{array}$

2. $\begin{array}{r} 1,338 \\ \times\ 45 \\ \hline \end{array}$

3. $\begin{array}{r} 343 \\ \times\ 78 \\ \hline \end{array}$

4. $\begin{array}{r} 3,333 \\ \times\ 76 \\ \hline \end{array}$

5. $\begin{array}{r} 4,127 \\ \times\ 28 \\ \hline \end{array}$

6. $\begin{array}{r} 245 \\ \times\ 18 \\ \hline \end{array}$

7. $\begin{array}{r} 2,706 \\ \times\ 92 \\ \hline \end{array}$

8. $\begin{array}{r} 2,156 \\ \times\ 39 \\ \hline \end{array}$

Name _____   Date _____

Whole Numbers: Multiplication

1. 982
   × 872

2. 2,775
   × 173

3. 1,615
   × 239

4. 594
   × 439

5. 2,138
   × 256

6. 1,953
   × 279

7. 187
   × 187

8. 658
   × 439

9. 3,126
   × 382

10. 1,759
    × 265

11. 2,274
    × 826

12. 565
    × 225

13. 284
    × 833

14. 2,408
    × 316

15. 3,946
    × 307

16. 477
    × 360

Whole Numbers: Multiplication

REMEMBER?
1234   1234
× 2468   × 2468

1. $\begin{array}{r} 1{,}243 \\ \times\ 2{,}286 \\ \hline \end{array}$ 2. $\begin{array}{r} 2{,}434 \\ \times\ 3{,}276 \\ \hline \end{array}$ 3. $\begin{array}{r} 1{,}432 \\ \times\ 3{,}266 \\ \hline \end{array}$

4. $\begin{array}{r} 3{,}681 \\ \times\ 4{,}532 \\ \hline \end{array}$ 5. $\begin{array}{r} 3{,}607 \\ \times\ 2{,}442 \\ \hline \end{array}$ 6. $\begin{array}{r} 3{,}245 \\ \times\ 4{,}318 \\ \hline \end{array}$ 7. $\begin{array}{r} 7{,}576 \\ \times\ 2{,}308 \\ \hline \end{array}$

8. $\begin{array}{r} 4{,}321 \\ \times\ 1{,}269 \\ \hline \end{array}$ 9. $\begin{array}{r} 4{,}433 \\ \times\ 2{,}247 \\ \hline \end{array}$ 10. $\begin{array}{r} 3{,}322 \\ \times\ 2{,}356 \\ \hline \end{array}$ 11. $\begin{array}{r} 8{,}764 \\ \times\ 3{,}148 \\ \hline \end{array}$

12. $\begin{array}{r} 3{,}836 \\ \times\ 4{,}103 \\ \hline \end{array}$ 13. $\begin{array}{r} 4{,}607 \\ \times\ 2{,}342 \\ \hline \end{array}$ 14. $\begin{array}{r} 3{,}439 \\ \times\ 3{,}636 \\ \hline \end{array}$ 15. $\begin{array}{r} 6{,}045 \\ \times\ 4{,}328 \\ \hline \end{array}$

Whole Numbers: Multiplication

A

1. $\begin{array}{r} 600 \\ \times\ 400 \\ \hline \end{array}$
2. $\begin{array}{r} 300 \\ \times\ 500 \\ \hline \end{array}$
3. $\begin{array}{r} 800 \\ \times\ 900 \\ \hline \end{array}$
4. $\begin{array}{r} 200 \\ \times\ 700 \\ \hline \end{array}$

5. $\begin{array}{r} 3{,}000 \\ \times\ 200 \\ \hline \end{array}$
6. $\begin{array}{r} 5{,}000 \\ \times\ 400 \\ \hline \end{array}$
7. $\begin{array}{r} 7{,}000 \\ \times\ 600 \\ \hline \end{array}$
8. $\begin{array}{r} 9{,}000 \\ \times\ 800 \\ \hline \end{array}$

B

1. $\begin{array}{r} 700 \\ \times\ 300 \\ \hline \end{array}$
2. $\begin{array}{r} 900 \\ \times\ 500 \\ \hline \end{array}$
3. $\begin{array}{r} 100 \\ \times\ 600 \\ \hline \end{array}$
4. $\begin{array}{r} 400 \\ \times\ 400 \\ \hline \end{array}$

5. $\begin{array}{r} 2{,}000 \\ \times\ 100 \\ \hline \end{array}$
6. $\begin{array}{r} 4{,}000 \\ \times\ 300 \\ \hline \end{array}$
7. $\begin{array}{r} 6{,}000 \\ \times\ 500 \\ \hline \end{array}$
8. $\begin{array}{r} 8{,}000 \\ \times\ 700 \\ \hline \end{array}$

Whole Numbers: Multiplication

A

1. 509
   × 402

2. 780
   × 430

3. 308
   × 360

4. 805
   × 906

5. 604
   × 208

6. 720
   × 305

7. 705
   × 104

8. 905
   × 540

- -

B

1. 408
   × 306

2. 340
   × 260

3. 707
   × 403

4. 600
   × 460

5. 702
   × 408

6. 680
   × 305

7. 503
   × 550

8. 903
   × 640

Whole Numbers: Multiplication

A

1. 3,700
× 208

2. 4,809
× 309

3. 4,570
× 300

4. 4,000
× 408

5. 6,205
× 800

6. 2,704
× 302

7. 5,079
× 320

8. 6,300
× 909

B

1. 4,600
× 309

2. 5,708
× 407

3. 5,460
× 500

4. 6,000
× 703

5. 7,304
× 700

6. 3,850
× 603

7. 6,088
× 430

8. 7,200
× 606

Whole Numbers: Multiplication

SKILL 6

1. 428
    × 70

2. 743
    × 40

3. 7,631
    × 50

4. 2,843
    × 90

SKILL 7

5. 4,736
    × 500

6. 6,208
    × 700

7. 5,289
    × 800

8. 5,074
    × 900

SKILL 8

9. 35,308
    × 2,000

10. 43,727
    × 7,000

11. 67,461
    × 8,000

12. 86,562
    × 9,000

Name _____   Date _____

Whole Numbers: Multiplication

SKILL 9

13. 37
   × 44

14. 66
   × 35

15. 59
   × 94

16. 78
   × 29

17. 93
   × 45

SKILL 10

18. 1,330
   × 94

19. 2,373
   × 90

20. 1,489
   × 74

21. 4,067
   × 75

SKILL 11

22. 6,502
   × 284

23. 4,063
   × 274

24. 6,455
   × 3,635

25. 5,864
   × 2,734

SKILL 12

26. 2,600
   × 200

27. 6,000
   × 470

28. 7,200
   × 570

29. 3,007
   × 306

Whole Numbers: Multiplication

SKILL 1

1. $\begin{array}{r} 6 \\ \times\, 4 \\ \hline \end{array}$
2. $\begin{array}{r} 9 \\ \times\, 3 \\ \hline \end{array}$
3. $\begin{array}{r} 5 \\ \times\, 7 \\ \hline \end{array}$
4. $\begin{array}{r} 7 \\ \times\, 8 \\ \hline \end{array}$
5. $\begin{array}{r} 6 \\ \times\, 9 \\ \hline \end{array}$

SKILL 2

6. $\begin{array}{r} 14 \\ \times\, 2 \\ \hline \end{array}$
7. $\begin{array}{r} 23 \\ \times\, 3 \\ \hline \end{array}$
8. $\begin{array}{r} 42 \\ \times\, 2 \\ \hline \end{array}$
9. $\begin{array}{r} 133 \\ \times\, 3 \\ \hline \end{array}$
10. $\begin{array}{r} 221 \\ \times\, 4 \\ \hline \end{array}$

SKILL 3

11. $\begin{array}{r} 17 \\ \times\, 4 \\ \hline \end{array}$
12. $\begin{array}{r} 15 \\ \times\, 5 \\ \hline \end{array}$
13. $\begin{array}{r} 12 \\ \times\, 5 \\ \hline \end{array}$
14. $\begin{array}{r} 114 \\ \times\, 7 \\ \hline \end{array}$
15. $\begin{array}{r} 313 \\ \times\, 8 \\ \hline \end{array}$

SKILL 4

16. $\begin{array}{r} 84 \\ \times\, 4 \\ \hline \end{array}$
17. $\begin{array}{r} 53 \\ \times\, 6 \\ \hline \end{array}$
18. $\begin{array}{r} 28 \\ \times\, 7 \\ \hline \end{array}$
19. $\begin{array}{r} 75 \\ \times\, 5 \\ \hline \end{array}$
20. $\begin{array}{r} 67 \\ \times\, 3 \\ \hline \end{array}$

SKILL 5

21. $\begin{array}{r} 207 \\ \times\, 6 \\ \hline \end{array}$
22. $\begin{array}{r} 816 \\ \times\, 2 \\ \hline \end{array}$
23. $\begin{array}{r} 3{,}142 \\ \times\, 5 \\ \hline \end{array}$
24. $\begin{array}{r} 8{,}627 \\ \times\, 9 \\ \hline \end{array}$

SKILL 6

25. $\begin{array}{r} 20 \\ \times\, 50 \\ \hline \end{array}$
26. $\begin{array}{r} 80 \\ \times\, 40 \\ \hline \end{array}$
27. $\begin{array}{r} 243 \\ \times\, 30 \\ \hline \end{array}$
28. $\begin{array}{r} 376 \\ \times\, 60 \\ \hline \end{array}$
29. $\begin{array}{r} 1{,}257 \\ \times\, 90 \\ \hline \end{array}$

Name _____ Date _____

Whole Numbers: Multiplication

SKILL 7

30. $\begin{array}{r} 303 \\ \times\ 500 \\ \hline \end{array}$ 31. $\begin{array}{r} 143 \\ \times\ 200 \\ \hline \end{array}$ 32. $\begin{array}{r} 6{,}148 \\ \times\ 400 \\ \hline \end{array}$ 33. $\begin{array}{r} 5{,}040 \\ \times\ 700 \\ \hline \end{array}$

SKILL 8

34. $\begin{array}{r} 2{,}123 \\ \times\ 4{,}000 \\ \hline \end{array}$ 35. $\begin{array}{r} 5{,}104 \\ \times\ 5{,}000 \\ \hline \end{array}$ 36. $\begin{array}{r} 36{,}227 \\ \times\ 3{,}000 \\ \hline \end{array}$ 37. $\begin{array}{r} 76{,}532 \\ \times\ 3{,}000 \\ \hline \end{array}$

SKILL 9

38. $\begin{array}{r} 14 \\ \times\ 13 \\ \hline \end{array}$ 39. $\begin{array}{r} 37 \\ \times\ 30 \\ \hline \end{array}$ 40. $\begin{array}{r} 62 \\ \times\ 26 \\ \hline \end{array}$ 41. $\begin{array}{r} 77 \\ \times\ 82 \\ \hline \end{array}$ 42. $\begin{array}{r} 48 \\ \times\ 65 \\ \hline \end{array}$

SKILL 10

43. $\begin{array}{r} 219 \\ \times\ 23 \\ \hline \end{array}$ 44. $\begin{array}{r} 487 \\ \times\ 15 \\ \hline \end{array}$ 45. $\begin{array}{r} 3{,}213 \\ \times\ 34 \\ \hline \end{array}$ 46. $\begin{array}{r} 6{,}040 \\ \times\ 67 \\ \hline \end{array}$

SKILL 11

47. $\begin{array}{r} 376 \\ \times\ 18 \\ \hline \end{array}$ 48. $\begin{array}{r} 764 \\ \times\ 82 \\ \hline \end{array}$ 49. $\begin{array}{r} 2{,}072 \\ \times\ 234 \\ \hline \end{array}$ 50. $\begin{array}{r} 4{,}354 \\ \times\ 2{,}132 \\ \hline \end{array}$

SKILL 12

51. $\begin{array}{r} 200 \\ \times\ 300 \\ \hline \end{array}$ 52. $\begin{array}{r} 504 \\ \times\ 400 \\ \hline \end{array}$ 53. $\begin{array}{r} 7{,}000 \\ \times\ 205 \\ \hline \end{array}$ 54. $\begin{array}{r} 8{,}200 \\ \times\ 502 \\ \hline \end{array}$

Name _____   Date _____

STUDENT PROGRESS CHART

Strand 3: Whole Numbers: Multiplication

Inventory

Score:_____ of 12

Skill 1

Page 1:_____ of 34
Page 2:_____ of 29
Page 3:_____ of 29
Page 4:_____ of 29
Page 5:_____ of 30
Page 6:_____ of 48
Page 7:_____ of 48

Skill 2

Page 1:_____ of 29
Page 2:_____ of 28
Page 3:_____ of 29

Skill 3

Page 1:_____ of 29
Page 2:_____ of 29
Page 3:_____ of 28

Skill 4

Page 1:_____ of 29
Page 2:_____ of 29
Page 3:_____ of 29
Page 4:_____ of 30

Skill 5

Page 1:_____ of 28
Page 2:_____ of 28
Page 3:_____ of 29
Page 4:_____ of 23
Page 5:_____ of 24
Review 1–5:_____ of 29

Skill 6

Page 1:_____ of 29
Page 2:_____ of 29
Page 3:_____ of 28
Page 4:_____ of 29
Page 5:_____ of 24
Page 6:_____ of 24

Skill 7

Page 1:_____ of 23
Page 2:_____ of 23
Page 3:_____ of 23

Skill 8

Page 1:_____ of 17
Page 2:_____ of 17
Page 3:_____ of 17

Skill 9

Page 1:_____ of 19
Page 2:_____ of 19
Page 3:_____ of 20
Page 4:_____ of 20

Skill 10

Page 1:_____ of 18
Page 2:_____ of 18
Page 3:_____ of 18
Page 4:_____ of 15
Page 5:_____ of 16

Skill 11

Page 1:_____ of 15
Page 2:_____ of 16
Page 3:_____ of 15

Skill 12

Page 1:_____ of 16
Page 2:_____ of 16
Page 3:_____ of 16
Review 6–12: _____ of 29
Cumulative
   Review: _____of 54